Acknowledgements

The author would like to thank the following colleagu
family members for their help and support during the writing and
production of this publication:

Eliza Johnson, Dahira Khalid, Roger Townsend, Sihao Zhou, Maciek
Sarara, David and Erika Evans and Tatsuo Nishimura.

Mark Evans has been a teacher for about 25 years. He has taught in
Australia, Japan, Malaysia and the UK. He graduated in languages
from University College London and has a PGCE, CELTA, DELTA,
Diploma in ESOL, as well as an MA in English Language Teaching. He
currently lives in London where he teaches at a college and a
university.

This edition published in London, England in 2018

ISBN- 13: 978-1717066831 (createspace assigned)

ISBN- 10: 1717066836

Text copyright @2018, Mark Evans

MeEducation

Please feel free to contact the author at - meeducation@yahoo.com

Visit the website at https://meeducation.net.

Table of Contents

Adjectives 1

Match the adjectives with their definition:

	Short
	Suitable
	Gives you benefits
	Able to move quickly and easily
	Very simple with no luxury
	Polite/showing respect
	Loveable
	Angry/worried
	Untidy with lots of objects
	In great pain
	Worried
	Proudly refusing to obey
	Helping others even if it causes you harm
	Lacking/not enough
	Not clever

adorable	agile	agitated	agonizing
altruistic	apt	austere	beneficial
brief	cluttered	concerned	courteous
defiant	deficient	dim-witted	

Exercise

Insert the most appropriate adjective into the space below:

1) The new kitten was so cute and _____.

2) The pain of her broken knee-cap was _____.

3) Tom always helped people without ever expecting a reward; he was very _____.

4) There was not enough sunlight in the tenement so the girl was _____ in vitamin D, which made her bones weak and brittle.

5) The monkey was so _____ that it could climb up the steep ravine effortlessly.

6) Henry's bedroom was _____ with books and toys everywhere.

7) Mr Fish's Vienna trip was very _____; only two hours.

8) Steve found the extra lessons very _____ and he became top of the class.

9) The passengers became very _____ as they had been stranded on the train for nearly three hours.

10) The Smith family had no money so they were compelled to lead a very _____ lifestyle.

11) The general was in a _____ mood as he refused to obey his superiors.

12) As the headmistress was so kind and _____ to all her pupils, she was immensely popular.

Adjectives 2

Match the adjectives with their definition:

	Very embarrassing
	Active and full of determination
	Very funny
	Extremely happy
	Huge
	Intended to look great and important
	Brightly coloured and easily seen
	Cheerful and not worried about the future
	Affected by magic
	Careful using only a little food/money
	Smells nice
	Unusual and exciting from a faraway country
	Horrible
	Confused and upset
	Believes anything

ecstatic	enchanted	exotic	feisty
flamboyant	flustered	fragrant	frugal
gargantuan	grandiose	grotesque	gullible
happy-go-lucky	hilarious	humiliating	

Exercise

Insert the most appropriate adjective into the space below:

1) Running a marathon in the freezing cold was an absolutely _____ task.

2) That comedian was totally _____.

3) The wizard lived in an _____ castle.

4) It was _____ when my trousers fell down in front of all my friends.

5) Sue believes anything; she's totally _____

6) Being a chef is hard work. They are very busy in the kitchen and are often _____.

7) She's a _____ girl; nothing ever bothers her and she always has a smile on her face.

8) When Steve won the jackpot in the lottery he was absolutely _____.

9) The face of the fire demon was _____.

10) The Jones family had very little money and so they lived a very _____ life.

11) She always wore _____ clothes so everyone could notice her easily.

12) The roses in the garden were very _____ .

Adjectives 3

Match the adjectives with their definition:

	Very thirsty
	Respected and admired
	Tired of doing so often
	Spotless/perfect
	Smells stale
	Believes anything because of little experience
	Peeved, really angry
	Chilly/rather cold
	Comes out at night
	Enthusiastic
	Very small amount/not enough
	Do what you are told
	Mildly funny
	Average quality
	Positive

immaculate   jaded   keen   light-hearted

livid   measly   mediocre   musty

naïve   nippy   nocturnal   obedient

optimistic   parched   prestigious

Exercise

Insert the most appropriate adjective into the space below:

1) It's _____ outside. Wear a warm jacket.

2) Philip was a very funny man, always making _____ jokes.

3) Last night's meal was not fantastic, just _____. I don't think I'll go back there again.

4) Monica wants to study hard. She is a very _____ pupil.

5) He used to be a very funny comedian but now he is tired and _____.

6) When Tim knocked over the antique vase his mother was absolutely _____.

7) They toiled all day in the meadows under the scorching sun but they only received a _____ amount of money.

8) Hamilton Hall is a very old stately home. Therefore, when you go inside there is a very _____ smell.

9) Bats are _____ creatures.

10) Oxford is one of the most _____ universities in the world.

11) As Mr Smith was such a strict teacher, the students were very _____.

12) You need to consume a great deal of water in the Australian desert to avoid becoming _____.

Adjectives 4

Match the adjectives with their definition:

	Use money carefully
	Strong and not likely to break
	Empty; available for use
	Likely to vomit
	Very important
	Say something but mean opposite
	Rich
	Do dangerously without caring about risks
	Unusual in a humorous way
	Serious and sad
	Huge
	Feeling sad and guilty
	Involves a lot of sudden changes/movement
	Make something complicated look easy
	Only one of something

queasy   reckless   remorseful   robust

sarcastic   simplistic   sombre   thrifty

turbulent   unique   vacant   vital

well-off   whopping   zany

Exercise

Insert the most appropriate adjective into the space below:

1) Twickenham is a very _____ area with many rich people.

2) The sign on the toilet door said "_____."

3) After telling a lie and being found out, the little boy felt very _____.

4) He is a _____ driver and has had several car crashes this year alone.

5) The brand new fence was very _____; it could stand up to anything.

6) The funeral was a very _____ occasion, with many of his relatives grieving.

7) It is _____ that you dry your hands before touching electricity.

8) Sue and Earl have a very _____ relationship; they are always quarrelling.

9) The Peterson family are not well-off so they have to be very _____.

10) The severe turbulence in the airplane just after she had eaten made her feel _____.

11) Matthew told a _____, great, big lie.

12) The Earth is _____; there is no other place like it in the universe.

Adjective Exercise 1

Put adjectives in the sentence to make them more interesting:

1) The boy walked in the park with his dog.

2) The girl saw a bear in the woods.

3) The cat saw a bird and climbed the tree.

4) The man had a dispute with his neighbour over the hedge.

5) The spaceman landed on the planet.

6) Steve ran across the meadow away from the bull.

7) Ken finished his work and went to his house.

8) Liz looked at the man. Then the man looked at his dog.

9) After the day she went to her bed.

10) Having run a marathon, they had a meal and a drink.

Adjective Exercise 1

Adjective Exercise 2

Put adjectives in the sentence to make them more interesting:

1) James ran home from the park as the sun set.

2) The pupils did their homework on the tram.

3) The merchant sold his wares in the market.

4) Dina perused the pamphlet in the hall.

5) Gary called his friend on the phone.

6) The undertaker received calls in his office.

7) The pirate took a swig of rum from a glass.

8) The lodger slept in his bed.

9) Having aroused his men with his speech, the king went to the fort.

10) The orphan lamented that his mother had died.

Alliteration 1

Put the most appropriate alliterative adjective before the nouns:

aching animated ambitious agile avaricious angelic adorable

_____ antelope, _____ arm, _____ Arnold

barren beloved bulky beneficial bewitched bountiful bossy

_____ boy, _____ bag, _____ beach

curious cantankerous chubby creepy cultured catastrophic

_____ cat, _____ caterpillar, _____ cowboy

deadly demonic defiant damp discrete dismal dreary

_____ door, _____ den, _____ dungeon

edible eminent enchanted elaborate enlightened elegant

_____ eagle, _____ entrance, _____ Eric

flippant flimsy flawless flamboyant foolhardy feisty

_____ friend, _____ family, _____ foe

gleeful grotesque gullible gregarious grouchy grateful

_____ girl, _____ gremlin, _____ goat

happy-go-lucky humungous harmonious hospitable harsh

_____ harp, _____ horse, _____ hiker

Exercise

Make 8 alliterative sentences using each letter from the previous page:

1)...

....

2)...

....

3)...

....

4)...

....

5)...

....

6)...

....

7)...

....

8)...

....

Alliteration 2

Put the most appropriate alliterative adjective before the nouns:

| ignorant | impeccable | impish | incompatible | insidious | intrepid |

_____ Eddie,   _____ elf,   _____ entrance

| jaded | jittery | jovial | jubilant | jealous | jagged | jolly |

_____ giraffe,   _____ general,   _____ janitor

| kind-hearted | knowledgeable | keen | knobbly |

_____ knees,   _____ gnome,   _____ kid

| lanky | livid | luxurious | lonesome | loathsome | lavish |

_____ lumberjack,   _____ labourer,   _____ lunch

| measly | mediocre | modest | murky | mundane | muffled |

_____ meal,   _____ mansion,   _____ Monday

| naïve | needy | nocturnal | nautical | nifty | nutritious |

_____ neighbour,   _____ Nicola,   _____ ninja

| obedient | oily | obese | ornate | outrageous | old-fashioned |

_____ office,   _____ official,   _____ opponent

| paltry | perky | phony | plump | prestigious | pristine | punctual |

_____ pool,   _____ peasant,   _____ pupil

Exercise

Make 8 alliterative sentences using each letter from the previous page:

1)...

....

2)...

....

3)...

....

4)...

....

5)...

....

6)...

....

7)...

....

8)...

....

Alliteration 3

Put the most appropriate alliterative adjective before the nouns:

| quaint quarrelsome queasy quintessential quirky quixotic |

_____ question, _____ queen, _____ quality

| radiant ragged regal remorseful rigid repulsive rundown |

_____ rock, _____ railway, _____ rogue

| serene sociable soggy stupendous sturdy sweltering shrill |

_____ Sunday, _____ summer, _____ servant

| tangible tedious thrifty tremendous traumatic turbulent |

_____ time, _____ Tuesday, _____ trip

| ultimate unkempt unsightly unruly unwieldy urban |

_____ uncle, _____ umbrella, _____ uniform

| vacant vengeful vulnerable vibrant vivid vigorous vague |

_____ van, _____ voyage, _____ victim

| warm-hearted well-groomed well-off wiggly witty wry |

_____ woman, _____ worm, _____ workman

| yapping yearning yucky yummy youthful zany |

_____ youth, _____ yob, _____ zebra

Exercise

Make 8 alliterative sentences using each letter from the previous page:

1)..

....

2)..

....

3)..

....

4)..

....

5)..

....

6)..

....

7)..

....

8)..

....

Adverbs 1

Match the adverbs with their definition:

	Quickly and energetically
	By chance
	Keep forgetting to do things
	Confusing and difficult to understand/choose
	With energetic interest
	Saying "yes"/showing agreement
	On purpose
	Frightening and violent
	Extremely happily
	Taking yourself too seriously
	Completely
	Unsurely
	Angrily
	Exactly and clearly
	Working well

absentmindedly   affirmatively   bewilderingly   blissfully

briskly   coincidentally   crossly   deliberately

doubtfully   earnestly   efficiently   enthusiastically

entirely   explicitly   ferociously

Exercise

Insert the most appropriate adverb into the space below:

1) As he was in a hurry, Basil walked _____ along the promenade.

2) Steve was very diligent and always studied _____.

3) German cars have a reputation for working _____.

4) Although Ralph denied breaking the window, his mother didn't believe his story and looked at him _____.

5) They had just tied the knot and were _____ in love.

6) Winning the lottery was _____ unexpected.

7) As George hadn't done the homework, his teacher scolded him _____.

8) "You're right!" Simon nodded _____.

9) Although his mother had _____ warned him not to go into the water, Dave went against her wishes.

10) Sue was _____ lost in the maze at Hampton Court.

11) The Doberman barked at the intruder _____.

12) As Rachel was in a bad mood, she was _____ obnoxious to Mark.

Adverbs 2

Match the adverbs with their definition:

	Unpleasantly
	Very happily
	Showing fear/worry
	Jokingly
	Like something very much
	Can't be doubted
	Do something regularly
	Hugely
	Seriously/correctly
	Curiously
	Do something unwillingly
	Enthusiastically
	Easily angry
	Having no clear order/plan
	Funnily

fondly	formally	frantically	grimly
grudgingly	habitually	haphazardly	humorously
immensely	indubitably	inquisitively	irritably
	jovially	jubilantly	keenly

Exercise

Insert the most appropriate adverb into the space below:

1) He went for a swim _____ every morning.

2) After passing the test he cheered _____.

3) When John dropped the priceless vase his wife looked at him very _____.

4) "Why did you come to the UK?" the immigration officer asked _____.

5) After setting up a successful business, he became _____ rich.

6) He was dressed very _____ for the job interview.

7) Down to the last five minutes in the exam, David worked _____ to finish his essay in time.

8) He always loved welcoming friends to his house and greeted them _____.

9) It was a joke and meant to be taken _____.

10) Rio organised his study notes _____. As a corollary he got a low grade and his parents were furious.

11) He knew all the answers to his teacher's questions and _____ put his hand up.

12) He was a man of honour and always taken _____ by his fellow professors.

Adverbs 3

Match the adverbs with their definition:

	Forcefully/energetically
	Very rude and unpleasantly
	Softly/affectionately
	Causing a deep or sharp feeling of sadness
	Like a machine
	Quickly
	Unusually, in a nice or interesting way
	Not worrying about pain caused to others
	Very sadly
	Occasionally
	Secretly
	Suggesting something unpleasant may happen
	Unclearly
	Unwillingly
	Positively

mechanically	miserably	obnoxiously	ominously
optimistically	periodically	poignantly	quirkily
reluctantly	ruthlessly	stealthily	swiftly
tenderly	vaguely	vigorously	

Exercise

Insert the most appropriate adverb into the spaces below:

1) The black storm clouds appeared _____ in the sky above the beach as an indication of impending doom.

2) In a desperate attempt not to be seen, the ninja crept _____ across the rooftops in the moonlight.

3) Although he hated studying, David _____ did his homework.

4) The kidnapper _____ pointed the gun at the hostages and demanded money.

5) Melanie _____ stroked the cat with a smile in her eyes.

6) _____ a blue moon appears in the sky at night.

7) It was a bright sunny day and James started his first day at work _____.

8) Ella _____ remembered her dream from last night.

9) She performed her job _____; she worked like a robot.

10) The boxer hit the punch bag _____.

11) He tried hard for the Tiffin test but he failed _____, just getting ten per cent.

12) Hannah ran _____ across the pasture.

Adverb Exercise 1

Put adverbs in the sentence to make them more interesting:

1) Eliza ran for the boat but it sailed off.

2) Steve walked through the labyrinth just as the ramparts appeared.

3) They looked up and saw the gremlin growling at them.

4) Shaun looked at the grubby façade and grinned.

5) The dictator nodded and sent the men screaming to the dungeon.

6) Nicola raised the amulet above her head and chanted.

7) The rebels assembled in the copse then marched into battle.

8) The boy sobbed and then rectified his mistake.

9) Having swigged the rum, Long John Silver drew his cutlass.

10) Gary rested his arms on the flimsy table and watched it collapse.

Adverb Exercise 2

Put adverbs in the sentence to make them more interesting:

1) David walked down the steps and looked at the dome.

2) The fugitive eluded the police for a fortnight but gave himself up.

3) All his limbs ached as he staggered towards the bullion.

4) The galleon sailed across the Channel and the crew cheered.

5) Luca typed on the keyboard then handed his homework in.

6) Nancy read the tome and put it down on the sturdy table.

7) After the final curtain the audience clapped and the actors bowed.

8) At the Bolshoi, the ballerinas danced and then fell to the ground.

9) The priest delivered his sermon from the pulpit while the audience listened.

10) Richard wiped his eyes and gazed at his insolent son.

Useful Vocabulary 1

Match the words with their definitions:

	Send someone away and not allow to return
	Short
	Want to get to the top
	Make someone believe something untrue
	Hug
	Nothing can grow there
	Give all of your time/energy to something
	Force someone to do something
	Loud and unpleasant long-lasting noise
	Choose a representative
	Feel very sad about something that happened
	Connected with a house
	Great danger
	Connected with countryside
	Someone who buys and sells goods
	Die from hard conditions
	Lazy; not working
	First person to do something
	Container/ship
	Sea journey
	Wealthy

ambitious	banish	barren	brief
compel	deceive	devote	din
domestic	elect	embrace	grieve
idle	merchant	peril	perish
pioneer	prosperous	rural	vessel	voyage

Exercise

Put the new words into the gaps in the correct grammatical form:

1) _____ life is much more tranquil than urban life.

2) The _____ set sail on her maiden voyage.

3) The peninsula was totally _____; nothing grew at all.

4) Tim's speech was very _____; it was over in two minutes.

5) At the children's party there was such a _____ that the police were called by anxious neighbours.

6) The discovery of precious metal made them very _____.

7) As Paula had done absolutely no work the whole holiday, her mum called her _____.

8) He was an _____ boy who wanted to get to the top.

9) After hearing about the death of her kitten, Erica _____ for over a week.

10) Mum does all the _____ chores while dad goes out to work.

11) Due to the political scandal, the people _____ a new president.

12) Colin was a prosperous _____ who sold his wares to many consumers.

13) The couple _____ for the last time as Lilly was about to board the train.

14) Although he was reluctant, David was _____ to study maths every day.

15) The Wright brothers were _____ in their field. They went on to invent the aeroplane.

Useful Vocabulary 2

Match the words with their definitions:

	Person who helps/supports you
	Ridiculous in an amusing way
	Stick/attach firmly to something
	Use something/someone for a purpose
	Weak/very little strength
	On time
	Particular and distinctive smell
	Disaster
	Become worse in condition/quality
	Enemy
	Productive
	Cure/solution
	Pierce/make a small hole in something
	Strong disapproval/disagreement of something
	Rarely
	Home
	Boring
	Fat/solid
	Connected with city
	Walk around for pleasure
	Done quickly

absurd	adhere	ally	calamity
deteriorate	employ	feeble	fertile
foe	odour	oppose	prompt
punctual	puncture	ramble	remedy
residence	seldom	stout	tedious urban

Exercise

Put the new words into the gaps in the correct grammatical form:

1) Many people _____ the terrible new development on the seafront.

2) Losing the match was an absolute _____ for the team as they had been a very ambitious side.

3) Having not eaten for days, his health started to_____.

4) Java in Indonesia has very _____ soil; anything can grow there.

5) They _____ on the hiking trails in the barren wilderness.

6) Sitting at home all day can be very _____.

7) There was a terrible _____ coming from the loft.

8) Far from being foes, the USA and the UK are strong _____.

9) Jake was a model pupil; he always _____ to the rules.

10) Ralph _____ servants to do the domestic chores as he was too idle.

11) Foxes can often be seen in the _____ environment.

12) The tranquil silence was _____ by a loud boom.

13) He perished because a _____ could not be found.

14) The thought of him wearing a clown costume to the dinner party was _____.

15) Jean was a prosperous pioneer who lived in a palatial _____ in rural England.

Useful Vocabulary 3

Match the words with their definitions:

	Entry to a place; agree something is true
	Ask for something formally
	Applicant for something
	Get used to
	Gently persuade someone to do something
	Understand
	Partially burn and blacken
	Refuse/say no; gradually get worse
	A short trip to do a job
	Modern, current
	Chase someone/something
	Rude showing no respect
	Discuss something in a formal way
	Showing sadness/sorrow about something
	Doesn't follow the rules
	Unhappiness, wanting better treatment
	Holy speech
	Grow/develop well
	Shrink and dry up
	High
	Done in a hurry, often lacking care

accustom   admission   appeal   candidate
char   coax   comprehend   contemporary
debate   decline   discontent   errand
flourish   hasty   insolent   lament
lofty   pursue   rogue   sermon   wither

Exercise

Put the new words into the gaps in the correct grammatical form:

1) _____ to the exhibition was very expensive.

2) After the calamitous fire the beams of the house were _____.

3) Having hidden for a long time, the feeble puppy had to be _____ out of hiding.

4) In Parliament the politicians _____ the bill.

5) Jeff forgot to water the plants so they all _____ and died.

6) Sarah could not _____ what the man was saying due to his bad diction.

7) There were many _____ taking the exam.

8) With the abundance of food, rats _____ in the urban environment.

9) Although she came from France, Corinne was _____ to driving on the left in Britain.

10) Jill was _____ with the meal and the poor service.

11) He was too _____ in making decisions so there were always problems.

12) The police _____ the culprits down a narrow alleyway but failed to nab them.

13) Father Bergin delivered a _____ from his pulpit during Sunday mass.

14) He _____ to the judge to change his decision.

15) Tahira _____ that she had lost her passport.

Useful Vocabulary 4

Match the words with their definitions:

	Correct/change a mistake
	Anger
	Awaken, stir up
	Someone you spend time with
	Gather
	Damaged/something wrong
	Interested in
	Repeat/remember
	Lazy
	Made up of
	Arm or leg
	Not allowed
	Have no money at all/impoverished
	Escape
	Pointless
	Drink large amounts from cup/bottle quickly
	Strong and unlikely to be damaged
	Lodger/someone who rents
	Say unkind/insulting things to someone
	Holy writing
	Argument/disagreement

arouse	assemble	companion	consist
curious	destitute	dispute	elude
flawed	futile	indolent	limb
prohibit	recite	rectify	scripture
sturdy	swig	taunt	tenant	wrath

Exercise

Put the new words into the gaps in the correct grammatical form:

1) Concrete foundations ensured the structure was _____.

2) Ken was able to _____ the entire poem beautifully.

3) As the value of his shares declined, he lost a fortune and was _____.

4) The pirate had a _____ of rum to ease his lament.

5) The kitten was very _____ and went into every nook and cranny.

6) King Henry V gave a great speech which _____ his troops.

7) The disciples hastily _____ in the forest clearing for a sermon.

8) The two friends were close _____.

9) Having been _____ by the bullies, Sam ran home crying.

10) The bad workmanship by the cowboy builders was _____ by professionals.

11) Due to dangerous riptides, his father _____ him from swimming in the bay.

12) The river was swiftly overflowing its banks, so putting up resistance was _____.

13) The fugitive had _____ the police for over a fortnight.

14) Water _____ of oxygen and hydrogen.

15) The neighbours had a big _____ about who should fix their broken fence.

Review 1 *(use the vocabulary from 1-4)*

Across	**Down**
2. Danger	1. Rarely
3. Tall	4. Enemy
5. Lazy	6. Job
7. Wake up	8. Countryside
9. Smell	10. Get worse
11. Rude	13. City
12. Grow	14. Die
15. Rich	16. Drink
17. A body part	19. Follow
18. An argument	
20. They pay a landlord	

Useful Vocabulary 5

Match the words with their definitions:

	Can be eaten
	Dirty
	Avoid
	Natural home of plants/animals
	Puzzled/confused
	Enthusiastically strong belief about something
	Looks like
	Foolishness
	Comparing two alike things
	Cheating someone illegally/immorally
	Doesn't work well
	Morally bad/evil behaviour
	Turn away from what is right
	Child with no parents
	Come together
	Someone who rules with total power
	Small person
	Do without shame
	Someone who kills others' pleasure
	Something that brings bad luck
	No longer fresh

analogy	bemused	blatant	converge
depraved	deviate	dictator	edible
evade	fervent	folly	fraud
grubby	habitat	inefficient	jinx
killjoy	midget	orphan	resemble	stale

Exercise

Put the new words into the gaps in the correct grammatical form:

1) Many fish from the river are _____. They taste great.

2) This loaf of bread is yesterday's, so now it's _____.

3) As the factory was _____, it lost money and went bankrupt.

4) The White Nile and the Blue Nile _____ at Khartoum in Sudan.

5) Having played lacrosse in the park, her hands became very _____.

6) Prince Charles _____ his mother to an extent.

7) He ruled with absolute power. He was a _____.

8) The convict _____ the police by disguising as a woman.

9) Going to the gambling den every night was sheer _____.

10) The criminal had been forging banknotes for years and was finally convicted of _____ by the judge.

11) Norman had his plans set in stone and would not _____ from them in any way.

12) Winning the lottery proved to be a _____ as they have had appalling luck ever since.

13) Phil was asked the corollary of a complex sum and looked _____.

14) The man was a _____ believer in God and listened to the sermon at church attentively.

15) The decline of the bamboo forests in China has led to loss of _____ for the giant panda.

Useful Vocabulary 6

Match the words with their definitions:

	Feel or express grief or sorrow
	Give food/nutrition to
	Recognise
	Too many opponents
	Agile
	Care about people's feelings
	Plants/trees that are growing well/healthily
	Get less in size/volume
	Extreme physical/mental tiredness
	Don't have any energy
	Concerned, worried
	Abandoned, neglected
	Fallen into partial ruin or decay
	Something that is difficult, tiring and hard work
	Confusing
	Thickly covered with plants/weeds
	Untidy, careless in appearance/behaviour
	Thoughtful and quiet
	Rude and offensive
	Rotten
	Sounds or spoken in unvarying tone

apprehensive	arduous	acknowledge	baffling
derelict	diminish	dilapidated	fatigue
lethargic	lush	monotonous	mourn
nimble	nourish	outnumber	overgrown
pensive	rancid	sensitive	slovenly vulgar

Exercise

Put the new words into the gaps in the correct grammatical form:

1) The old buildings became _____ after the factories closed down in the recession.

2) Everyone _____ the passing away of their dear friend.

3) Ernest Shackleton had the _____ task of traversing South Georgia in appalling conditions.

4) Hiroko had worked too hard; she was overcome by _____.

5) The small British army was heavily_____ by thousands of Zulus at Rourke's Drift.

6) As they lived so far apart, the couple's love _____.

7) It was folly to eat the _____ butter as it was inedible.

8) He sat in the tranquil garden and was _____ about the future.

9) Earl could not comprehend the homework; it was _____.

10) Ken led a _____ lifestyle, never grooming himself or working.

11) The orphan was _____ about his first day at school.

12) The habitat was _____ with weeds and Japanese knotweed.

13) The teacher was so tedious as he spoke in a _____ voice.

14) No one liked Ed as he was blatantly rude and _____; reasoning with him was futile.

15) The enchanting valley was green and _____.

Useful Vocabulary 7

Match the words with their definitions:

	Understand
	Broken
	Bad tempered, often complaining
	Hit with a whip
	Morally very bad
	Stuck in a place
	Loud and rough
	Secret plan by group to do something bad
	Group of people who refuse to obey
	Become weakened
	Not as good as something
	Can't see clearly
	Do without thinking of consequences
	Duty, something you must do
	Look down on someone
	Different from each other
	Childish bad temper
	Eat quickly
	Statue/model of someone
	Work long and hard
	Growing/spreading uncontrollably

bleary	condescend	conspiracy	devour
diverse	effigy	fathom	lash
grouchy	heinous	inferior	kaput
marooned	mutiny	obligation	petulant
raucous	rampant	rash	toil	wane

Exercise

Put the new words into the gaps in the correct grammatical form:

1) He had just woken up and looked at him with _____ eyes.

2) After working badly for so long, the old contraption was finally _____.

3) Captain Blythe of the Bounty was so terrible that the crew decided to _____.

4) Chinese cuisine is very _____; there are lots of dishes.

5) As Ned was mumbling, they couldn't _____ out what he was saying.

6) The malnourished sailor was _____ on a desert island and becoming increasingly destitute.

7) Su Ling _____ every day for many years in the rice paddy.

8) As a result of old age, he lamented that his health was beginning to _____.

9) He was guilty of many _____ crimes.

10) The peasant was famished and _____ the bun swiftly.

11) Guy Fawkes led the _____ to blow up Parliament.

12) On November 5th people burn _____ of Guy Fawkes.

13) His decision to walk out on his job proved a rather _____ one.

14) Being aloof, he spoke to people in a _____ manner.

15) The vulgar cadet had been swigging gin heavily and was now loud and _____.

Useful Vocabulary 8

Match the words with their definitions:

	Save from destruction
	Don't give up
	Idea based on feeling not reason
	Hide/move slowly and secretly
	Make white
	Existing but not noticeable
	Decay/break down
	Rule in a hard/cruel way
	Curved inwards
	Helpless
	Angry as a result of injustice
	Short lasting smell
	Full of detail
	Small mistake/failure
	Start again after a pause
	Fondness for the past
	Become infected
	Someone who expects bad things
	Group of soldiers guarding where they live
	Something very big and ugly
	Violent disorder and confusion

bleach	concave	decompose	elaborate
fester	garrison	hunch	indignant
lame	lapse	latent	mayhem
monstrosity	nostalgia	oppress	pessimist
resume	salvage	skulk	tenacious	whiff

Exercise

Put the new words into the gaps in the correct grammatical form:

1) The smell of the water gave him _____ about his past.

2) After the skirmish the wounds on his limbs _____.

3) The crew hastily debated what they could _____ from the sinking ship.

4) Bob was a real _____; always worried about the future.

5) When he passed the abattoir he caught the _____ of decomposing animals.

6) The train driver had a _____ of concentration which led to the collision.

7) Stalin was a dictator and _____ many people during his rule of the Soviet Union.

8) The priest gave a sermon from a pulpit, which was very _____.

9) He was not sure but he had a _____ who the culprit was.

10) As the teacher was not present, there was _____ in the classroom.

11) The show _____ after the intermission.

12) The new building was so ugly people called it a _____.

13) After being falsely accused Ted felt _____.

14) It was futile to make Sue change her mind as she was as _____ as a bulldog.

15) There is a British army _____ based in Gibraltar.

Review 2 *(use the vocabulary from 5-8)*

Across
1. Smell
4. One tone
6. Different
8. Doesn't work
9. Get less
10. Stranded
14. Come together
16. Whiten
18. Detailed
19. Consume

Down
2. Understand
3. Thinking
5. Never give up
7. Continue
11. Similar to
12. Possible to eat
13. No energy
15. Moves easily
17. Not fresh

Useful Vocabulary 9

Match the words with their definitions:

	Move suddenly
	Funny/amusing
	Work involving great effort and difficulty
	Praise
	Fence made of stakes
	Job you learn & do many years
	Having great variety
	Think/talk contentedly about the past
	Someone who travels from place to place
	Food
	Very poor person
	Small hill of sand
	Happen again
	Person of high importance in a company
	Most typical
	Someone who is not good at sea travel
	Unpleasant and shocking
	Actor/connected with acting
	Disease caused by lack of vitamin C
	Line between two places
	Numerical fact

appalling	boundary	career	dune
executive	grub	jerk	jocular
landlubber	laud	multifarious	nomad
onerous	paling	pauper	quintessential
reminisce	recur	scurvy	statistic	thespian

Exercise

Put the new words into the gaps in the correct grammatical form:

1) Lack of vitamin C resulted in _____ among sailors so they took lemons to compensate for this.

2) The _____ between two countries is called a border.

3) He did the training course at work to enhance his _____.

4) Jock ate all the _____ and slovenly relaxed on the couch.

5) Having spent all his money on a lavish lifestyle, he was now a _____.

6) The pupils were _____ for being so well behaved.

7) Janet met her old school friends and _____ about the past.

8) The Maasai are a tribe of semi-_____ who live in Kenya.

9) Due to his _____ behaviour, Reg was grounded for over a fortnight.

10) He was a _____ person; always smiling.

11) Bluebells are a _____ English spring flower in woodland areas.

12) The car _____ suddenly and they were all thrown forward.

13) The sand _____ stretched for miles and miles in the barren landscape.

14) The _____ around the Georgian house were elaborate.

15) It was an _____ task but he could at last do it.

Useful Vocabulary 10

Match the words with their definitions:

	Drag something heavy
	Suggest rather than say directly
	Make unclear, confuse
	List of things to discuss at a meeting
	Things that remain to be done
	Scare deeply
	Go to attack and steal
	Accept defeat
	Brilliant and exciting
	Small cylindrical glass bottle
	Discourage
	Put shiny surface on
	Not reveal thoughts/feelings
	Prevent
	Incorrect
	Grassy plain in hot area
	Say sounds/words to communicate a feeling
	Upset, shock, confuse
	Showing strong feelings, passionate
	Wave hands/arms in air for expression
	Outburst of uncontrollable anger

agenda	backlog	capitulate	dishearten
erroneous	faze	gesticulate	glaze
haul	imply	maraud	obfuscate
petrify	phial	reticent	savannah
scintillating	tantrum	thwart	utter	vehement

Exercise

Put the new words into the gaps in the correct grammatical form:

1) The wizard poured the potion from the _____ on the bookcase.

2) Geoff was totally _____ by the difficult mathematical formula.

3) British forces in Singapore were forced to _____ to the advancing Japanese army.

4) When the insolent little boy couldn't get what he wanted he threw a _____.

5) Giraffes live on the _____ in Kenya.

6) Mules helped _____ the coal from the mines.

7) Having failed to get into the school of his choice, Ben was utterly _____.

8) There was a lot to discuss on the _____ of the meeting.

9) Mark said nothing in class; he was far too _____.

10) When the depraved Vikings landed in England they _____ local towns and villages.

11) The howl of the wolves in the pitch black _____ John.

12) "Help me!" _____ the old man with his dying breath.

13) Keith was a great thespian who liked to _____ when he played his part.

14) Having been on strike for two weeks, there was now a great _____ of work to do.

15) Trevor declined the _____ dish in the restaurant as it was not the one he ordered.

Useful Vocabulary 11

Match the words with their definitions:

	Having or showing learning
	Boost
	Happens irregularly
	Passionate, very enthusiastic
	Seize and hold on to
	Oneness, coming together
	Many things/people crowded together
	Overwhelming, discouraging
	Hard, bare, severe
	Give oneself pleasure
	Suggest something more than usual meaning
	Block out
	Cruel and insensitive
	Showing quiet dislike, unenthusiastic
	Style of music/literature
	Destroy completely
	Severe snowstorm
	Be able to put yourself in others' shoes
	Arrival of large number of people/things
	Kept within bounds/enclosed
	Welcoming to stranger

ardent   blizzard   callous   confined
connotation   daunting   dense   empathize
erudite   fillip   genre   grasp
hospitable   indulgent   influx   obliterate
obscure   sporadic   stark   sullen   unity

Exercise

Put the new words into the gaps in the correct grammatical form:

1) The impending storm meant the boats were _____ to their moorings.

2) Alaska has many appalling _____ in winter.

3) Bob was a very _____ man, having read a great many books.

4) The library stocked books of many _____.

5) The prospect of climbing Mount Everest was _____.

6) Sue didn't come to class on a regular basis; her attendance was

_____.

7) The large _____ of people into the stadium created such a din.

8) Having been in the same situation as Gary, I can really _____ with him.

9) Their view of the sea was _____ by the trees.

10) The _____ vegetation of the forest made it impenetrable.

11) The expensive chocolates were absolutely _____.

12) During the Blitz many houses in East London were _____.

13) Dahira and her family were always welcoming people into their home; they were very _____.

14) The money being invested as a result of the weak pound gave the economy a real _____.

15) The dismal winter weather made him a very _____ person.

Useful Vocabulary 12

Match the words with their definitions:

	Stylish and attractive
	Happens by (esp. lucky) chance
	Place where people/animals feel safe
	Book/film which is longer than others
	Zigzag/not direct
	Lazy with no interest
	Forced to stay and suffer in a bad place
	Skilful/clever in getting what you want
	Illegal
	On the edge
	Kid
	Bring back to life
	Demand noisily and angrily
	Someone who saves you
	Careless mistake
	Attack continuously with bombs/missiles
	Limitation, allowance
	Final demand
	Connected with money
	In bad condition
	Fanatical

artful	bombard	clamour	dashing
epic	financial	fortuitous	haven
illicit	languid	languish	meander
nipper	oversight	periphery	quota
rabid	revive	saviour	tatty	ultimatum

Exercise

Put the new words into the gaps in the correct grammatical form:

1) The path _____ down the hill to a set of imposing buildings.

2) The city was _____ by heavy artillery and many buildings were obliterated.

3) As they didn't like living in the city centre, they resided on the _____ of the city.

4) His old brief case was now looking very _____; he clearly needed a new one.

5) The port was a safe _____ for people fleeing conflict.

6) After his heart attack, the doctors desperately tried to _____ him.

7) Being well-groomed and in a new suit, Ted looked _____.

8) Mother Teresa was seen as a _____ of the poor.

9) During the war, each person received a weekly _____ of meat.

10) After investing huge sums of money in the stock market, Sid made significant _____ loses.

11) The Black Hole of Calcutta was an infamous jail where many people _____.

12) The pupils were famished and _____ on the canteen door.

13) The police were aware of the _____ activities in the area.

14) Spartacus was an _____ film set in ancient Rome.

15) Ellen was a _____ girl; she just laid on the sofa all day.

Review 3 *(use the vocabulary from 9-12)*

Across	Down
Across	**Down**
1. messy	2. terrible
5. attack	3. joking
6. long story	4. limit
8. pull	7. not happy
10. things to do	9. edge
12. wrong	11. educated
16. not lawful	13. remember
18. passionate	14. together
19. scare	15. say
20. type	17. food

Useful Vocabulary 13

Match the words with their definitions:

	Stop
	Communicate, express something
	Destruction and end of the world
	Powerful, impressive
	Style of clothing
	Throw someone legally out of a house
	Someone good at making speeches
	Wild and not civilised
	Laugh disrespectfully at someone
	Left pieces of something after destruction
	Want to harm others
	Become weaker and unable to continue
	Great enjoyment of something
	Very slight difference
	Very fashionable and expensive
	Defend yourself against defensive blows
	Short sleep
	Make someone suffer something bad
	Vocabulary
	Very eager to obey
	Not properly planned

apocalypse	barbarian	cease	chic
convey	debris	doze	evict
falter	formidable	garb	half-baked
inflict	jeer	lexis	malevolent
nuance	orator	parry	relish	servile

Exercise

Put the new words into the gaps in the correct grammatical form:

1) After eating a huge lunch Eva _____ off in the park.

2) The Robinsons were _____ from their abode as they could not pay their rent.

3) During the Cold War people warned of nuclear _____.

4) Ranjit looked dashing dressed in his Indian_____.

5) _____ entered Rome to maraud it and destroyed many relics in the process.

6) Completing the ascent of Ben Nevis was a _____ task.

7) All throughout the Blitz people hoped the bombardment would _____.

8) There was a lot of _____ washed up on the banks of the Thames.

9) The swordsmen were unfazed as they _____ each other's blows.

10) The audience _____ at the terrible performance of the heavy metal band.

11) When he opened the email he had also unwittingly downloaded a _____ virus.

12) They relished dining in the _____ new restaurant in Mayfair.

13) Having studied a great deal, Rex had a wide range of _____.

14) Bill loved giving speeches as he was a great _____.

15) Lucy _____ the thought of lying on a sun-kissed beach in Malaga for a fortnight.

Useful Vocabulary 14

Match the words with their definitions:

	Sum of money someone owes
	Make something nicer by decorating/adding to
	Refuse to buy something
	Lucky
	Criticize strongly
	Not interested in something
	Think about something all the time
	Angry about something
	An evil spirit that takes bodies from graves
	A serious crime
	Copy
	Desire to achieve your goals
	A soldier guarding an outside building
	Can't catch a particular disease
	Gain something (often) after hard work/plans
	Make a horse go quite fast
	Something in your way
	Small and unimportant
	Make something happen faster
	A large piece of cloth with a picture on
	Priest or minister

apathetic	aspire	boycott	canter
debt	embellish	felony	ghoul
hasten	immune	jammy	lambast
mimic	narked	obsessive	obstacle
parson	petty	reap	sentry	tapestry

Exercise

Put the new words into the gaps in the correct grammatical form:

1) The soldier stepped out of his _____ box and aimed his rifle.

2) While playing roulette, Ken was really _____ and won a small fortune.

3) Sue was training hard as she _____ to win a gold medal.

4) When the train was delayed the passengers became really

_____.

5) Erica's dress was _____ with gold sequins.

6) Due to the high prices, consumers decided to _____ the store.

7) The factory manager _____ the workers to produce more.

8) She was on trial for a number of _____ including armed robbery and murder.

9) After her jab, Rose was _____ to the disease.

10) The horse _____ across the savannah towards the sand dunes.

11) Being homeless and broke were just two of the _____ Jake had to overcome.

12) The Bayeux _____ was woven in France to commemorate the Battle of Hastings in 1066.

13) After the ultimatum had passed, Mr Stone was thrown into jail because he could not pay his large _____.

14) The _____ said mass every Sunday morning in the local church.

15) Fred _____ the rewards of all his arduous work and was now a prosperous man.

Useful Vocabulary 15

Match the words with their definitions:

	Kind of West Indian song
	In plenty/abundance of
	Sign representing something
	Uninteresting in appearance
	Distant in feeling, not friendly
	Complete failure
	Show or prove reason
	Small bar/restaurant
	Someone who is not accepted by a group
	Good luck charm
	Crowd of people
	Someone who loves their country
	Goods for sale
	No longer needed/unemployed
	Young, unmarried, noble woman
	Safe place
	Unsuitable, unrealistic
	Using more words than necessary
	Relatives
	Someone good at languages
	Shake/tremble

aloof	bistro	calypso	damsel
emblem	fiasco	galore	horde
impractical	justify	kin	linguist
merchandise	nondescript	outcast	patriot
quiver	redundant	sanctuary	talisman	verbose

Exercise

Put the new words into the gaps in the correct grammatical form:

1) The family darted across the bridge for _____ from the floods.

2) It was difficult to _____ why he had spent all the family money.

3) There was a great deal of _____ to purchase in the market.

4) _____ is a style of music that originated in Trinidad and Tobago in the Caribbean.

5) The puppy was cold and hungry and sat _____ in the corner.

6) They used to go to a chic little _____ in Main Street that had lovely wine.

7) Carol was a great _____ who could speak many languages.

8) _____ of warriors came running down the hill at the battle.

9) Eric was a great _____ who loved his country.

10) With the advent of mobile phones, few people used telephone boxes so they became _____.

11) Financially, the building of the Sydney Opera House was a complete _____ as it was delayed and over budget.

12) They lived in a _____ building in the suburbs which was hard to remember.

13) Bob was very _____ and it took him a long time to express himself clearly.

14) The _____ of Wales is a daffodil.

15) Eli was an _____ as she had nothing in common with anyone.

Useful Vocabulary 16

Match the words with their definitions:

	Sleep somewhere different
	Persuade someone to help/support you
	Something bad is going to happen soon
	Yellow-brown strong material
	Interrupt and embarrass someone speaking
	Someone who asks for food/money
	Recently made/designed
	Rise and float magically in the air
	Sudden memory of past experience
	Give particular time/money for something
	Small argument, usually between lovers
	Push/knock someone in a crowd
	Roughly built hut
	Mouth
	Organised public show
	Nonsense/foolishness
	Seriously injure someone
	Scold
	Make decisions sensibly
	Gets angry easily
	Someone who, uninvolved, watches something

allot	beggar	caper	doss
enlist	flashback	gob	heckle
impending	jostle	khaki	level-headed
levitate	maim	new-fangled	onlooker
pageant	quick-tempered	rebuke	shanty tiff

Exercise

Put the new words into the gaps in the correct grammatical form:

1) Eri and Ed made up after their lovers' _____ at a romantic spot.

2) Hordes of _____ gathered around to watch the pageant.

3) In the Rio slums there are a large number of _____ towns.

4) Bill used to be a _____ collecting money by the side of the road.

5) There was a _____ in the street and all the community participated.

6) While the politician was giving his speech the protesters started _____ him.

7) The soldiers looked formidable; all dressed in their _____ uniforms ready to go out on parade.

8) The crowd _____ each other to get to the front of the queue.

9) Graham _____ down on his friend's sofa because he missed the last train.

10) The magician _____ as part of his grand finale.

11) The teacher _____ time slots to each student for the tutorials.

12) He suffered _____ from the apocalyptic bombardment of his city.

13) Eliza was always calm and _____.

14) During the Cambodian civil war many people were _____ by land mines.

15) Barry went to the tuck shop and stuffed his _____ with grub.

Review 4 *(use the vocabulary from 13-16)*

<table>
<tr><td colspan="2">

Across
3. Copy
5. Deflect
7. Badly built hut
8. Money owed
10. Mouth
14. Injure
15. Sleep
16. Speaker
17. Vocab
18. Argument

</td><td>

Down
1. Family
2. Crowd
4. Stop
5. Not important
6. Criticize
9. Sign
11. Tremble
12. Distant
13. Guard
15. Sleep

</td></tr>
</table>

Useful Vocabulary 17

Match the words with their definitions:

	Strange and difficult to understand
	Slight idea about something
	State/period of inactivity/non-movement
	Throw something no longer needed away
	Farming
	Colour
	Force people to leave a place
	Easily broken
	Place where wild animal sleeps
	Proud in an annoying way
	Unusual person who behaves differently
	Blocked, full of traffic
	Punish
	Spoken not written
	Behaving in a loud way
	Related to marriage
	Seawater lake separated by rocks or sand
	Quick, violent hitting movement; beat
	Breaks down in environment
	Swamp
	Strange feeling something bad will happen

agriculture   biodegradable   congested   doldrums
enigma   fragile   gloat   hue
inkling   jettison   lair   lairy
lagoon   maverick   nuptial   oral
penalise   premonition   purge   quagmire   thrash

Exercise

Put the new words into the gaps in the correct grammatical form:

1) The sinking bird _____ its wings frantically in the water in a bid to stay afloat.

2) The _____ was truly impenetrable and they had no chance of traversing it.

3) In rural areas _____ is the main source of employment.

4) The students had an _____ French exam last week.

5) Due to the road works, there is heavy _____ in the centre of town.

6) One of the passengers had a _____ that the Titanic would sink.

7) He dared not venture into the _____ of the dreaded beast.

8) Her complexion was of a pale _____.

9) The Apollo rocket was designed to _____ its fuel tanks in orbit.

10) These days many plastic bags are designed to be _____.

11) There was a large _____ on the seafront where you could take a plunge.

12) The museum curator was careful when holding the Ming Dynasty vase as it was so _____.

13) After winning the prize, he _____ to all the people he had beaten.

14) The athlete was _____ for cheating in the race.

15) In Soviet Russia Stalin _____ his army to get rid of people he deemed undesirable.

Useful Vocabulary 18

Match the words with their definitions:

	Burn brightly
	Famous, well-respected and admired
	Something that spoils
	Go to a party uninvited
	Public official
	Good to eat
	Bullets, rockets, shells etc.
	Traitor
	Cross street carelessly
	Causing painful feeling
	Prevent from leaving
	Hospital for recovering people
	Combine two separate things
	Showing great care/attention to detail
	Grow again
	Procession of vehicles/riders
	Can be used for many different purposes
	Showing great wealth
	Attack someone making them look like a fool
	Make a solemn statement
	Asia

ammunition   blight   cavalcade   detain
flare   gate-crash   harrowing   illustrious
jaywalk   lampoon   meticulous   notary
opulent   Orient   palatable   quisling
regenerate   sanatorium   synthesis   testify   versatile

Exercise

Put the new words into the gaps in the correct grammatical form:

1) Carl Linnaeus _____ categorised all the plants and animals.

2) In India, due to lack of appropriate crossing points, it is common to _____.

3) The soldiers did not have enough _____ to repel the siege.

4) Betty worked at the court as a _____.

5) The concrete monstrosity _____ the entire neighbourhood.

6) Brian was _____ at work due to an impromptu meeting.

7) Singapore is one of the great cities of the _____.

8) The local cuisine is quite _____.

9) As Liz lit the match it _____ up in her face.

10) As a witness, she was called to court to _____.

11) Traumatised, the survivors of the crash spoke of their _____ story.

12) The Savoy is an _____ five star hotel in London's West End with no expense spared on its interior.

13) They were recovering from the virus in a _____.

14) Lord Nelson had an _____ career as a sailor.

15) Turmeric is a _____ herb that can be used in any dish to complement its flavour.

Useful Vocabulary 19

Match the words with their definitions:

	Thrown away by original owner
	Drop of liquid
	Formally bring to an end
	Start burning
	Small, dirty house/hut
	Spoil the surface of something
	Pay too much importance to petty things
	Involves very hard physical work
	Make someone very angry/agitated
	Behave in a typical manly way
	Do better than competitors
	Make laws
	Metal loops for a horse rider
	Speed
	Giving fair treatment to all sides
	Do just one part at a time uncoordinated
	Study hard
	Steep, deep, narrow valley
	Delicate skill
	Go back to former (worse) state
	Delay/postpone an action

abolish   backbreaking   cast off   deface
even-handed   finesse   globule   hovel
inflame   kindle   legislate   macho
nit-pick   outstrip   piece-meal   procrastinate
ravine   regress   stirrup   studious   tempo

Exercise

Put the new words into the gaps in the correct grammatical form:

1) They attempted to _____ the fire to keep warm in the park.

2) Tim went to the gym every day in an attempt to appear _____.

3) Slavery was officially _____ over two hundred years ago.

4) The company had no real strategy to repair the railways; it was all very _____.

5) As the climbers descended Mount Fuji, they came across a treacherous _____.

6) Working in the construction industry can be _____ work.

7) Eric was a fantastic darts player who often scored a bullseye with great _____.

8) He was such a pauper that he was forced to reside in a _____.

9) She took all her _____ to the charity jumble sale.

10) Simon and Sarah _____ about purchasing a new house due to the prohibitive cost.

11) David played the piano at just the right _____.

12) Vandals had _____ the statue with graffiti during the night.

13) Neville was a very _____ boy as he studied every day without fail.

14) As the politicians debated, passions were _____ by the controversial comments made.

15) Having not studied for such a long time, his maths level began to _____.

Useful Vocabulary 20

Match the words with their definitions:

	Say something without thinking
	Punish by hitting many times
	Pause when nothing happens
	Severe mental pain
	Attractive and exciting
	Great skill at doing something
	Catch/arrest
	Force something on someone
	Shows good judgement
	Dislike intensely
	Two words together that mean the opposite
	In very bad condition
	Speech/comment at end of book/play
	Connected with heat
	Small, white fungus
	Badly made with not enough care
	Look down on someone as inferior
	Fight back successfully; disgust
	Short journey
	Pay money back
	Annoying

anguish   blurt   canny   disdain
epilogue   flog   glamorous   hiatus
impose   jaunt   loathe   mildew
nab   oxymoron   pesky   prowess
reimburse   repel   run-down   shoddy   thermal

Exercise

Put the new words into the gaps in the correct grammatical form:

1) The inhabitants _____ the invaders as they tried to climb over the wall.

2) News of his death caused his wife great _____.

3) The _____ insects bothered him so much that he began to sob.

4) Gary always _____ out his opinion without thinking first.

5) With the loss of the steel mill, the area became _____.

6) In Roman times, if you broke the law, you were often _____.

7) "Deafening silence" is an excellent example of an _____.

8) The Scotsman was a _____ businessman who always got a good deal.

9) Eric _____ eating mushrooms; they made him feel sick

10) The ruthless dictator _____ his rules on the citizens without any consultation.

11) She was a _____ lady who always dressed like a princess.

12) The king was aloof and had great _____ for his subjects whom he regarded as peasants.

13) The damp walls of the pauper's hovel meant that _____ was growing everywhere.

14) He had a nondescript _____ flask to keep his tea warm.

15) She was desperately disappointed with the builder's _____ work and wanted it remedied immediately.

Review 5 _(use the vocabulary from 17-20)_

Across

3. Go back
4. Beast's home
5. Showing wealth
7. Colour
8. Attack
12. Spoil
14. Busy
15. Keep
16. Style
18. Small, bad house
19. Trip

Down

1. Careful
2. Speed
6. Beat
9. Arrest
10. Set alight
11. Badly done
13. Hate
14. Wise
17. Small idea

Senses Vocabulary 1

Taste	Smell	Touch	Sound	Sight

Put the vocabulary below in the appropriate column above:

Rancid	Acidic	Sensuous	Whine	Drone
Succulent	Fragrant	Cacophony	Vibrant	Yodel
Thundering	Damp	Stale	Zesty	Aromatic
Grotesque	Pungent	Tepid	Tender	Prattle
Velvety	Furry	Putrid	Piquant	Warble
Silky	Odour	Stench	Bitter	Scorching
Rustle	Noxious	Plop	Musty	Bray

Senses Vocabulary 2

Taste	Smell	Touch	Sound	Sight

Put the vocabulary below in the appropriate column above:

Chortle	Acrid	Fetid	Stuffy	Eyesore
Humid	Lukewarm	Deafening	Hideous	Coarse
Melodic	Brackish	Mildewed	Prickly	Dim
Sonorous	Translucent	Dank	Savoury	Gooey
Purring	Cute	Tart	Scented	Uneven
Resonant	Mature	Mute	Stagnant	Slimy
Gleaming	Dappled	Gritty	Astringent	Reek

Answer Key

Adjectives 1-4

Adjectives 1	Adjectives 2	Adjectives 3	Adjectives 4
Brief	Humiliating	Parched	Thrifty
Apt	Feisty	Prestigious	Robust
Beneficial	Hilarious	Jaded	Vacant
Agile	Ecstatic	Immaculate	Queasy
Austere	Gargantuan	Musty	Vital
Courteous	Grandiose	Naïve	Sarcastic
Adorable	Flamboyant	Livid	Well-off
Agitated	Happy-go-lucky	Nippy	Reckless
Cluttered	Enchanted	Nocturnal	Zany
Agonizing	Frugal	Keen	Sombre
Concerned	Fragrant	Measly	Whopping
Defiant	Exotic	Obedient	Remorseful
Altruistic	Grotesque	Light-hearted	Turbulent
Deficient	Flustered	Mediocre	Simplistic
Dim-witted	Gullible	Optimistic	Unique
1 adorable	1 gargantuan	1 nippy	1 well-off
2 agonising	2 hilarious	2 light-hearted	2 vacant
3 altruistic	3 enchanted	3 mediocre	3 remorseful
4 deficient	4 humiliating	4 keen	4 reckless
5 agile	5 gullible	5 jaded	5 robust
6 cluttered	6 flustered	6 livid	6 sombre
7 brief	7 happy-go-lucky	7 measly	7 vital
8 beneficial	8 ecstatic	8 musty	8 turbulent
9 agitated	9 grotesque	9 nocturnal	9 thrifty
10 austere	10 frugal	10 prestigious	10 queasy
11 defiant	11 flamboyant	11 obedient	11 whopping
12 courteous	12 fragrant	12 parched	12 unique

Alliteration 1-3

Various combinations

Adverbs 1-3

Adverbs 1	Adverbs 2	Adverbs 3
Briskly	Grimly	Vigorously
Coincidentally	Jubilantly	Obnoxiously
Absentmindedly	Frantically	Tenderly
Bewilderingly	Jovially	Poignantly
Enthusiastically	Fondly	Mechanically
Affirmatively	Indubitably	Swiftly
Deliberately	Habitually	Quirkily
Ferociously	Immensely	Ruthlessly
Blissfully	Formally	Miserably
Earnestly	Inquisitively	Periodically
Entirely	Grudgingly	Stealthily
Doubtfully	Keenly	Ominously
Crossly	Irritably	Vaguely
Explicitly	Haphazardly	Reluctantly

Efficiently	Humorously	Optimistically
1 briskly	1 habitually	1 ominously
2 enthusiastically	2 jubilantly	2 stealthily
3 efficiently	3 irritably	3 reluctantly
4 doubtfully	4 inquisitively	4 ruthlessly
5 blissfully	5 immensely	5 tenderly
6 entirely	6 formally	6 periodically
7 crossly	7 frantically	7 optimistically
8 affirmatively	8 fondly	8 vaguely
9 explicitly	9 humorously	9 mechanically
10 bewilderingly	10 grudgingly	10 vigorously
11 ferociously	11 keenly	11 miserably
12 deliberately	12 indubitably	12 swiftly

Useful Vocabulary 1-5

Useful Vocabulary 1	Useful Vocabulary 2	Useful Vocabulary 3	Useful Vocabulary 4	Useful Vocabulary 5
Banish	Ally	Admission	Rectify	Edible
Brief	Absurd	Appeal	Wrath	Grubby
Ambitious	Adhere	Candidate	Arouse	Evade
Deceive	Employ	Accustom	Companion	Habitat
Embrace	Feeble	Coax	Assemble	Bemused
Barren	Punctual	Comprehend	Flawed	Fervent
Devote	Odour	Char	Curious	Resemble
Compel	Calamity	Decline	Recite	Folly
Din	Deteriorate	Errand	Indolent	Analogy
Elect	Foe	Contemporary	Consist	Fraud
Grieve	Fertile	Pursue	Limb	Inefficient
Domestic	Remedy	Insolent	Prohibit	Depraved
Peril	Puncture	Debate	Destitute	Deviate
Rural	Oppose	Lament	Elude	Orphan
Merchant	Seldom	Rogue	Futile	Converge
Perish	Residence	Discontent	Swig	Dictator
Idle	Tedious	Sermon	Sturdy	Midget
Pioneer	Stout	Flourish	Tenant	Blatant
Vessel	Urban	Wither	Taunt	Killjoy
Voyage	Ramble	Lofty	Scripture	Jinx
Prosperous	Prompt	Hasty	Dispute	Stale
1 rural	1 oppose	1 admission	1 sturdy	1 edible
2 vessel	2 calamity	2 charred	2 recite	2 stale
3 barren	3 deteriorate	3 coaxed	3 destitute	3 inefficient
4 brief	4 fertile	4 debated	4 swig	4 converge
5 din	5 rambled	5 withered	5 curious	5 grubby
6 prosperous	6 tedious	6 comprehend	6 aroused	6 resembles
7 idle	7 odour	7 candidates	7 assembled	7 dictator
8 ambitious	8 allies	8 flourished	8 companions	8 evaded
9 grieved	9 adhered	9 accustomed	9 taunted	9 folly
10 domestic	10 employed	10 discontented	10 rectified	10 fraud
11 elected	11 urban	11 hasty	11 prohibited	11 deviate
12 merchant	12 punctured	12 pursued	12 futile	12 jinx
13 embraced	13 remedy	13 sermon	13 eluded	13 bemused
14 compelled	14 absurd	14 appealed	14 consists	14 fervent
15 pioneers	15 residence	15 lamented	15 dispute	15 habitat

Useful Vocabulary 6-10

Useful Vocabulary 6	Useful Vocabulary 7	Useful Vocabulary 8	Useful Vocabulary 9	Useful Vocabulary 10
Mourn	Fathom	Salvage	Jerk	Haul
Nourish	Kaput	Tenacious	Jocular	Imply
Acknowledge	Grouchy	Hunch	Onerous	Obfuscate
Outnumber	Lash	Skulk	Laud	Agenda
Nimble	Heinous	Bleach	Paling	Backlog
Sensitive	Marooned	Latent	Career	Petrify
Lush	Raucous	Decompose	Multifarious	Maraud
Diminish	Conspiracy	Oppress	Reminisce	Capitulate
Fatigue	Mutiny	Concave	Nomad	Scintillating
Lethargic	Wane	Lame	Grub	Phial
Apprehensive	Inferior	Indignant	Pauper	Dishearten
Derelict	Bleary	Whiff	Dune	Glaze
Dilapidated	Rash	Elaborate	Reoccur	Reticent
Arduous	Obligation	Lapse	Executive	Thwart
Baffling	Condescend	Resume	Quintessential	Erroneous
Overgrown	Diverse	Nostalgia	Landlubber	Savannah
Slovenly	Petulant	Fester	Appalling	Utter
Pensive	Devour	Pessimist	Thespian	Faze
Vulgar	Effigy	Garrison	Scurvy	Vehement
Rancid	Toil	Monstrosity	Boundary	Gesticulate
Monotonous	Rampant	Mayhem	Statistic	Tantrum
1 derelict	1 bleary	1 nostalgia	1 scurvy	1 phial
2 mourned	2 kaput	2 festered	2 boundary	2 obfuscated
3 arduous	3 mutiny	3 salvage	3 career	3 capitulate
4 fatigue	4 diverse	4 pessimist	4 grub	4 tantrum
5 outnumbered	5 fathom	5 whiff	5 pauper	5 savannah
6 diminished	6 marooned	6 lapse	6 lauded	6 haul
7 rancid	7 toiled	7 oppressed	7 reminisced	7 disheartened
8 pensive	8 wane	8 elaborate	8 nomads	8 agenda
9 baffling	9 heinous	9 hunch	9 appalling	9 reticent
10 slovenly	10 devoured	10 mayhem	10 jocular	10 marauded
11 apprehensive	11 conspiracy	11 resumed	11 quintessential	11 petrified
12 overgrown	12 effigies	12 monstrosity	12 jerked	12 uttered
13 monotonous	13 rash	13 indignant	13 dunes	13 gesticulate
14 vulgar	14 condescending	14 tenacious	14 palings	14 backlog
15 lush	15 raucous	15 garrison	15 onerous	15 erroneous

Useful Vocabulary 11-15

Useful Vocabulary 11	Useful Vocabulary 12	Useful Vocabulary 13	Useful Vocabulary 14	Useful Vocabulary 15
Erudite	Dashing	Cease	Debt	Calypso
Fillip	Fortuitous	Convey	Embellish	Galore
Sporadic	Haven	Apocalypse	Boycott	Emblem
Ardent	Epic	Formidable	Jammy	Nondescript
Grasp	Meander	Garb	Lambast	Aloof
Unity	Languid	Evict	Apathetic	Fiasco
Dense	Languish	Orator	Obsessive	Justify
Daunting	Artful	Barbarian	Narked	Bistro
Stark	Illicit	Jeer	Ghoul	Outcast
Indulgent	Periphery	Debris	Felony	Talisman

Connotation	Nipper	Malevolent	Mimic	Horde
Obscure	Revive	Falter	Aspire	Patriot
Callous	Clamour	Relish	Sentry	Merchandise
Sullen	Saviour	Nuance	Immune	Redundant
Genre	Oversight	Chic	Reap	Damsel
Obliterate	Bombard	Parry	Canter	Sanctuary
Blizzard	Quota	Doze	Obstacle	Impractical
Empathize	Ultimatum	Inflict	Petty	Verbose
Influx	Financial	Lexis	Hasten	Kin
Confined	Tatty	Servile	Tapestry	Linguist
Hospitable	Rabid	Half-baked	Parson	Quiver
1 confined	1 meanders	1 dozed	1 sentry	1 sanctuary
2 blizzards	2 bombarded	2 evicted	2 jammy	2 justify
3 erudite	3 periphery	3 apocalypse	3 aspired	3 merchandise
4 genres	4 tatty	4 garbs	4 narked	4 calypso
5 daunting	5 haven	5 barbarians	5 embellished	5 quivering
6 sporadic	6 revive	6 formidable	6 boycott	6 bistro
7 influx	7 dashing	7 cease	7 hastened	7 linguist
8 empathize	8 saviour	8 debris	8 felonies	8 hordes
9 obscured	9 quota	9 parried	9 immune	9 patriot
10 dense	10 financial	10 jeered	10 cantered	10 redundant
11 indulgent	11 languished	11 malevolent	11 obstacles	11 fiasco
12 obliterated	12 clamoured	12 chic	12 tapestry	12 nondescript
13 hospitable	13 illicit	13 lexis	13 debt	13 verbose
14 fillip	14 epic	14 orator	14 parson	14 emblem
15 sullen	15 languid	15 relished	15 reaped	15 outcast

Useful Vocabulary 16-20

Useful Vocabulary 16	Useful Vocabulary 17	Useful Vocabulary 18	Useful Vocabulary 19	Useful Vocabulary 20
Doss	Enigma	Flare	Cast off	Blurt
Enlist	Inkling	Illustrious	Globule	Flog
Impending	Doldrums	Blight	Abolish	Hiatus
Khaki	Jettison	Gate-crash	Kindle	Anguish
Heckle	Agriculture	Notary	Hovel	Glamorous
Beggar	Hue	Palatable	Deface	Prowess
New-fangled	Purge	Ammunition	Nit-pick	Nab
Levitate	Fragile	Quisling	Backbreaking	Impose
Flashback	Lair	Jaywalk	Inflame	Canny
Allot	Gloat	Harrowing	Macho	Loathe
Tiff	Maverick	Detain	Outstrip	Oxymoron
Jostle	Congested	Sanatorium	Legislate	Rundown
Shanty	Penalise	Synthesise	Stirrup	Epilogue
Gob	Oral	Meticulous	Tempo	Thermal
Pageant	Lairy	Regenerate	Even-handed	Mildew
Caper	Nuptial	Cavalcade	Piece-meal	Shoddy
Maim	Lagoon	Versatile	Studious	Disdain
Rebuke	Thrash	Opulent	Ravine	Repel
Level-headed	Biodegradable	Lampoon	Finesse	Jaunt
Quick-tempered	Quagmire	Testify	Regress	Reimburse
Onlooker	Premonition	Orient	Procrastinate	Pesky
1 tiff	1 thrashed	1 meticulously	1 kindle	1 repelled
2 onlookers	2 quagmire	2 jaywalk	2 macho	2 anguish
3 shanty	3 agriculture	3 ammunition	3 abolished	3 pesky

4 beggar	4 oral	4 notary	4 piece-meal	4 blurted
5 pageant	5 congestion	5 blighted	5 ravine	5 run-down
6 heckling	6 premonition	6 detained	6 backbreaking	6 flogged
7 khaki	7 lair	7 Orient	7 finesse	7 oxymoron
8 jostled	8 hue	8 palatable	8 hovel	8 canny
9 dossed	9 jettison	9 flared	9 cast offs	9 loathed
10 levitated	10 biodegradable	10 testify	10 procrastinated	10 imposed
11 allotted	11 lagoon	11 harrowing	11 tempo	11 glamorous
12 flashbacks	12 fragile	12 opulent	12 defaced	12 disdain
13 level-headed	13 gloated	13 sanatorium	13 studious	13 mildew
14 maimed	14 penalised	14 illustrious	14 inflamed	14 thermal
15 gob	15 purged	15 versatile	15 regress	15 shoddy

Senses vocabulary 1

Taste	Smell	Touch	Sound	Sight
Acidic	Rancid	Succulent	Thundering	Grotesque
Stale	Fragrant	Velvety	Rustle	Vibrant
Piquant	Damp	Silky	Cacophony	
Bitter	Pungent	Damp	Plop	
Zesty	Odour	Furry	Whine	
	Noxious	Sensuous	Drone	
	Putrid	Tepid	Yodel	
	Stench	Tender	Prattle	
	Zesty	Scorching	Warble	
	Musty		Bray	
	Aromatic			
	Stale			

Senses vocabulary 2

Taste	Smell	Touch	Sound	Sight
Brackish	Acrid	Humid	Chortle	Gleaming
Mature	Fetid	Lukewarm	Melodic	Translucent
Tart	Mildewed	Gritty	Sonorous	Cute
Savoury	Dank	Prickly	Purring	Dappled
	Stuffy	Coarse	Resonant	Hideous
	Scented	Gooey	Mute	Eyesore
	Stagnant	Uneven	Dim	Dim
	Astringent	Slimy	Deafening	
	Reek			

Printed in Great Britain
by Amazon

78973110R00045